Express Yourself

by Amy Leggett-Caldera

PEARSON

Glenview, Illinois • Boston, Massachusetts
Chandler, Arizona • Upper Saddle River, New Jersey

We can express ourselves in many ways.

These friends are talking to each other. We can use our words to show our feelings.

We can dance to express ourselves. These dancers are moving their bodies. People dance in many ways. Dancing is fun!

We can play music to express ourselves.

These drummers are playing drums. They beat drums with their hands. What are other ways to make music?

We can make art to express ourselves.

This artist is painting a picture. She uses a paintbrush. She paints to show her feelings. People love to look at art.

We can write to express ourselves. You can share your writing or keep it to yourself.

This writer is sad. He is writing about his feelings in his journal.

We can sing to express ourselves.
There are sad and happy songs.
These singers are singing a silly song.
What songs do you sing?

We express ourselves in many ways.
Each way is special.

How do you express yourself?